CELTIC
MANDALAS

26 INSPIRING DESIGNS PLUS 10 BASIC
TEMPLATES FOR COLOURING AND MEDITATION

LISA TENZIN-DOLMA

WATKINS PUBLISHING

LONDON

CELTIC SPIRITUALITY

THE ANCIENT CELTS, WHO FLOURISHED THROUGHOUT EUROPE DURING THE FIRST MILLENNIUM BC, WERE RENOWNED AS WARRIORS, STORYTELLERS AND CRAFTSPEOPLE. THE BELIEFS AND TRADITIONS OF THE CELTS HAVE BEEN PASSED DOWN TO US THROUGH MANY LEGENDS, BUT ARE PERHAPS BEST PRESERVED AND DEPICTED IN SYMBOLIC ARTWORK. CELTIC IMAGERY CAN PROVIDE WONDERFUL INSIGHT INTO CELTIC SPIRITUALITY.

The Celts, or Keltoi as the ancient Greeks named them, were a group of tribes and clans who spread westwards across Europe from the Danube as far as Spain, France and the British Isles. In Classical Greek and Roman literature, stories abound of the Celts in battle: their warlike reputation, dyed hair and tattooed bodies terrified their adversaries.

But the Celts were a spiritual people as well. Intrinsic to their beliefs was the idea that three was the most sacred and magical number. Celtic tales, therefore, often contain references to groups of three people, animals or significant events, while Celtic art, as well as the mandalas in this book, often contains groups of three objects, such as spirals or animal forms, to intensify the symbolic power of the images. The Celts regarded life itself as a three-part cycle of birth, growth and death; and they worshipped the Triple Earth Goddess in the forms of the young, innocent Maiden, the kind, nurturing Mother and the wise old Crone.

Celtic legends were also populated by magical beings who had the power to bless or curse, and by heroes such as Cúchulainn and Bran, whose long voyages on the Western Sea led them to deepen their knowledge of the world and themselves. This often involved visiting the Otherworld – the land of the dead – where they were required to face all sorts of trials.

From the earliest times, Celtic artefacts reveal the people's passionate engagement with the spiritual world. One of the oldest symbols they depicted was the Sun – the giver of all life. With the coming of the Iron Age from around 600BC, the Celts cultivated talented metal-workers within their communities. Their richly crafted jewelry, vessels and weapons still featured primal symbols, such as the sun-wheel, but now they also included elegant, stylized plant and animal forms, and depictions of heroes and heroines, gods and goddesses, and much more.

Richly decorated artefacts were often buried with the dead. In the royal burial chambers of the central European Celts, the deceased were sent to the next life with valuable weapons and ornaments, many of which were adorned with animal shapes or zig-zag designs.

"I ARISE TODAY / THROUGH A MIGHTY STRENGTH, /
THE INVOCATION OF THE TRINITY."

THE DEER'S CRY (ANON.)

(C.9TH CENTURY AD)

"THAT HE WAS VERSED IN MAGIC IS TRUE, FOR HE
WAS EVER KNOWN AS THE KNOWLEDGEABLE MAN . . .
FOR HE HAD EATEN THE SALMON OF KNOWLEDGE."

THE BOYHOOD OF FIONN (ANON.)

(12TH CENTURY)

"THE WHOLE OF CREATION AND LIFE, AS IT
MANIFESTS, IS THE EFFECT OF THE OLD GOD
BEING TRANSMUTED INTO A NEW ONE."

TRADITIONAL CELTIC TEACHING

(2ND CENTURY BC — 1ST CENTURY AD)

"I BATHE THY PALMS / IN SHOWERS OF WINE, /
IN THE LUSTRAL FIRE, / IN THE SEVEN ELEMENTS."

INVOCATION OF THE GRACES (ANON.)

(1ST CENTURY BC)

The Green Man is a pre-Christian image associated with spring and nature, and is a symbol of rebirth.
Some contend that the Green Man is a male counterpart to Gaia – the Earth Mother, or Great
Goddess. It is believed that certain figures from popular legends are derived from the archetype
of the Green Man – most notably, in the Arthurian tale of *Sir Gawain and the Green Knight.*

The Celts also used these types of designs to embellish their clothes and to tattoo their bodies, and they extended this art style to their stonework. One of the most distinctive features of Celtic art – its intricate knotwork – developed in Britain and Ireland with the advent of Christianity, arising from a fusion of Celtic and Germanic styles. Crosses with knotwork designs – which are believed to represent eternity and interconnectedness – were carved from stone and forged in metal, and became a regular feature of Christian religious manuscripts.

The mandalas displayed in this book beautifully encapsulate the ancient power and wisdom of Celtic symbols within the framework of traditional Eastern mandalas. The simplest mandala is the circle, which symbolizes wholeness in fact, the word *mandala* is Sanskrit for "circle". While mandalas are not strictly typical of Celtic tradition, it seems fitting to bring the two things together, as the circle has deep spiritual resonance in Celtic art, as a symbol of infinity and the unending cycle of life.

When selecting a mandala in this book to colour in and use for meditation, just opt for one that appeals really strongly to you. All the mandalas are presented as line drawings. The first 26 designs, which are complex and sophisticated, are followed by a selection of basic geometrical templates you can elaborate to create your own design. Once you have chosen your mandala, let the recommended colour palette guide you in deciding how to colour it in; or alternatively, choose your own colours, following your intuition. When your mandala is coloured to your personal preference, you can begin your meditation.

Meditation relies heavily on concentration, so before using a mandala that you have coloured in, find a quiet place to sit, far from distractions or noise. Try to absorb the peaceful atmosphere around you. Then use the following step-by-step guide as a prompt to good practice.

HOW TO MEDITATE ON MANDALAS

1. With the chosen mandala placed on a table or on the floor at arm's length in front of you, perhaps on an improvised easel, level with your eye-line, sit comfortably – either on a chair with your feet flat on the floor, or on a cushion with your legs crossed.

2. Breathe slowly and deeply, from the diaphragm, while emptying and stilling your mind.

3. Gently gaze at the mandala and relax your eyes so that, initially, the image goes slightly out of focus.

4. Sitting quietly, concentrate fully on the image and allow its shapes, patterns and colours to work on your unconscious mind. If distracting thoughts arise, let them drift away and bring your focus back to the mandala.

5. Do this for at least 5 minutes initially. In later sessions, gradually try to build up your meditation period to 15 minutes.

6. When you are ready, slowly bring your attention back to the world around you.

DRAGON POWER

TO THE CELTS THE FIGURE OF THE DRAGON SYMBOLIZED BOTH THE POWER OF NATURE AND THE IMPORTANCE OF RECOGNIZING AND PROTECTING OUR OWN HIDDEN POWERS AND RESOURCES.

1 Focus on the two intertwined dragons in the centre of the mandala. Think of them as representing your deepest and most precious thoughts, feelings, beliefs and capacities – your "hidden treasure". Know that this treasure is always there for you to draw upon.

2 Shift your attention to the space around the dragons. View this as your sacred space, where you can feel safe in the world. Protect this with all your heart and soul, and allow yourself to go there any time you need to rest, recuperate and be regenerated.

3 Finally, look at the dragons in the outer circle. As you watch them dance around the mandala, over and through the knotted loops of life, consider how they might symbolize the part of you that others see. Appreciate how this "outer self" is supported and sustained by the strong and vibrant "inner self".

RECOMMENDED COLOUR PALETTE

INTERTWINED DRAGONS: **Red** for passion, strength, lust;
Yellow for warmth, confidence, joy, balance
SPACE AROUND DRAGONS: **Green** for nature, fertility, charity, prosperity, health
OUTER BACKGROUND: **Blue** for tranquillity, protection, devotion, sincerity

"NOT OF MOTHER OR FATHER WAS MY CREATION.
I WAS MADE FROM THE NINEFOLD ELEMENTS."

TALIESIN

(C.534—C.599 AD)

SEVEN SPIRALS

IN CELTIC LORE THE NUMBER SEVEN WAS ASSOCIATED WITH
AN INCREASE IN GOOD FORTUNE. THE SEVEN SPIRALS AT THE
CENTRE OF THIS MANDALA ENCOURAGE YOU TO OPEN YOUR HEART
AND WELCOME LOVING ENERGY INTO YOUR LIFE.

1 Let your gaze rest on the seven central spirals. Feel light and life-giving warmth radiating from their swirling energy, as if from the sun. Know in your heart that, whatever your situation, all will be well.

2 Shift your focus to the knotwork around the central circle. Let the interweaving path remind you that every event in life leads to new connections and exciting possibilities.

3 Move outward to the spirals in the square border. Let their colourful pattern open your spirit to inspiration, even in the firm grounding of daily life.

4 Finally, consider the outer ring of tiny bright circles – symbolic of your positive, joyful inner self.

RECOMMENDED COLOUR PALETTE

SEVEN CENTRAL SPIRALS: **Blue** for tranquillity, protection, devotion, sincerity; **Green** for nature, fertility, charity, prosperity, health; **Purple** for power, piety, sanctity, sentimentality

KNOTWORK: **Green** for nature, fertility, charity, prosperity, health; **Purple** for power, piety, sanctity, sentimentality

SPIRALS IN SQUARE BORDER: **Green** for nature, fertility, charity, prosperity, health; **Purple** for power, piety, sanctity, sentimentality; **Yellow** for warmth, confidence, joy, balance

TINY CIRCLES: **Green** for nature, fertility, charity, prosperity, health; **Yellow** for warmth, confidence, joy, balance

"AN ENCHANTED WORLD IS ONE THAT SPEAKS TO THE SOUL, TO THE MYSTERIOUS DEPTHS OF THE HEART AND IMAGINATION WHERE WE FIND VALUE, LOVE AND UNION WITH THE WORLD."

THOMAS MOORE

(1779—1852)

TREE OF LIFE

THE CELTS VIEWED TREES AS A CONNECTION
BETWEEN THE EARTHLY WORLD AND THE HIGHER REALMS:
A SOURCE OF GREAT SPIRITUAL NOURISHMENT AND GROWTH.
LET THE TREE OF LIFE BOTH GROUND AND INSPIRE YOU.

1 Focus softly on the circle of roots at the mandala's centre: the secret place from which life springs. Imagine that you, too, have roots, which connect you with the centre of the Earth. Gain strength and a sense of safety from being so firmly anchored.

2 View the flourishing branches of the four trees, all stemming from the same small core of roots. Recognize that you, like the trees, can blossom and grow – both emotionally and spiritually – as long as you remain firmly grounded.

3 Widen your focus to take in the whole mandala. Look beyond the square, which stands for the stability of the physical world, to the birds, which symbolize your connection with the spiritual realm. Know that your spirit, like the birds, can soar high and free.

RECOMMENDED COLOUR PALETTE

ROOTS: **Blue** for tranquillity, protection, devotion, sincerity
BRANCHES: **Green** for nature, fertility, prosperity, health, rootedness
BIRDS: **Yellow** for warmth, confidence, joy, balance

"IT IS THE TIMBER OF POETRY THAT WEARS MOST SURELY, AND THERE IS NO TIMBER THAT HAS NOT STRONG ROOTS AMONG THE CLAY AND WORMS."

JOHN MILLINGTON SYNGE

(1871—1909)

CUP OF PLENTY

CELTIC LEGENDS TELL OF THE MAGICAL CUP OR
CAULDRON OF PLENTY, WHICH CAN NEVER BE EMPTIED AND
WHICH GIVES ANYONE WHO TOUCHES IT THEIR HEART'S DESIRE.
THIS CUP IS A SYMBOL OF THE LIMITLESS GIFTS OF THE UNIVERSE.

1   Focus softly on the bejewelled cup at the centre of the mandala. Its magic works through the power of love and gratitude – think of the people or things that you feel blessed to have in your life.

2   Shift your eyes to the overflowing liquid, and the pool of swirling, life-enriching waters that it creates all around. Recognize this as the gift of infinite abundance, and open your mind to a sense of its limitlessness. Know that you will always be able to find or bring about whatever you most need.

3   Move your gaze out to the outer circle of intertwined chain-links. As you accept that your needs will be fulfilled, the links of trust both in yourself and in the benevolence of the universe will grow stronger.

RECOMMENDED COLOUR PALETTE

CUP: **Orange** for encouragement, attraction, kindness, plenty
BACKGROUND: **Green** for nature, fertility, charity, prosperity, health
OUTER CIRCLE: **Purple** for power, piety, sanctity, sentimentality, with **Yellow** (standing in for gold) for
energy, wealth, intelligence, longevity

"I DRAW MY WISDOM FROM THE RENOWNED CAULDRON.
THE BREATH OF NINE MUSES KEEPS IT BOILING."

FROM A WELSH ARTHURIAN TALE

BIRDS OF INSPIRATION

IN CELTIC BELIEF BIRDS ARE MESSENGERS OF THE GODS –
INSPIRING CREATURES THAT ENCOURAGE YOU TO LIVE FREELY,
FULLY AND COMPASSIONATELY.

1 Focus softly on the intertwined birds at the centre of this mandala. Feel their strength, sharp-sightedness and grace awaken the same qualities in you.

2 Next, take your focus to the four coiled birds positioned just inside the outermost band of the mandala. Feel the birds' swirling energy and let your spirit soar.

3 Now, direct your attention to the eight herons around the edge of the mandala, which are Celtic symbols of enduring love. Allow your mind to quieten and absorb their gentle intelligence, so that you can bring their compassion to your interactions with others.

RECOMMENDED COLOUR PALETTE

CENTRAL BIRDS: **Blue** for tranquillity, protection, devotion, sincerity;
White for purity, concentration, meditation, peace
SMALLER OUTER BIRDS: **Blue** for tranquillity, protection, devotion, sincerity
CENTRAL BACKGROUND: **Red** for passion, strength, lust, fertility
OUTER BACKGROUND: **Yellow** for warmth, confidence, joy, balance

"OUR INNER TRUTH IS AS BRIGHT AS THE FOAM CAST UP BY A MIGHTY WAVE,
AS THE SHEEN OF A SWAN IN SUNLIGHT, AS THE COLOUR OF SNOW ON A MOUNTAIN."

ADAPTED FROM AN EARLY IRISH TEXT

TRIPLE SPIRAL

THE TRIPLE SPIRAL REPRESENTS THE ETERNAL CYCLE OF BIRTH,
DEATH AND REBIRTH, AND THE INTERCONNECTEDNESS OF MIND,
BODY AND SPIRIT. FOCUSING ON THIS SYMBOL HELPS YOU TO FLOW
IN HARMONY WITH THE RHYTHM OF LIFE.

1   Look at the triple spiral at the centre of the mandala, and recognize it as the continual life cycle within you. At every instant, cells are being born, doing their work, dying and being replaced; similarly, thoughts constantly arise in, and pass from, your mind.

2   Next, bring your attention to the smaller triple spirals around the outside of the central motif. Imagine them flowing into one another and let your mind, body and spirit merge in harmony with them.

3   Shift your gaze further out to the straight edges of the mandala, which hold and stabilize the spirals' power within a square. Know that you can gain strength from this solid base – particularly in times of great change.

RECOMMENDED COLOUR PALETTE

TRIPLE SPIRAL: **Blue** for tranquillity, protection, devotion, sincerity; **Yellow** for warmth, confidence,
joy, balance; with **Green** lining for nature, fertility, charity, prosperity, health
BACKGROUND SPIRAL PATTERN: As above

"THE UNIVERSE ITSELF SHALL BE OUR IMMORTALITY!"

OSCAR WILDE

(1854—1900)

CELTIC CROSS 1

THE CELTIC CROSS REPRESENTS THE UNION OF HEAVEN AND EARTH, OR OF MASCULINE AND FEMININE. THIS MANDALA CAN THEREFORE HELP YOU TO UNIFY OPPOSING FORCES WITHIN YOUR LIFE AND TO LIVE MORE HARMONIOUSLY.

1 Begin by focusing gently on the cross. See the dense knotwork within it as symbolic of the tightly woven threads of your life, as you interact with everyone and everything around you. Cherish these connections.

2 Next, shift your gaze to the interlacing curves at the centre, where the "limbs" of the cross meet. See this loose pattern as representative of the flowing energy at the calm core of your being – where there is space for all elements of your life to coexist peacefully.

3 Now consider the mandala as a whole. Feel the balance between the traditional masculine solidity of the external square and the more fluid feminine power of the circles. Strive to achieve a similar balance in your approach to any problems that arise in life: a healthy combination of firmness and gentleness.

RECOMMENDED COLOUR PALETTE

KNOTWORK: **Blue** for tranquillity, protection, devotion, sincerity
CIRCULAR FRAME and SQUARE FRAME: **Yellow** for warmth, confidence, joy, balance
CENTRAL INTERLACING CURVES: **Blue** for tranquillity, protection, devotion, sincerity;
with an **Orange** background for encouragement, attraction, kindness, plenty
BLANK SPACES IN CIRCLE: **Black** for strength, wisdom, vision, success
BLANK SPACES IN SQUARE: **Red** for passion, courage, lust, fertility

"I KNOW MY GOD CREATES THE WISEST PROPHETS.
I KNOW THE HAZEL OF POETRY. I KNOW THE MIGHTY GOD."

ADAPTED FROM THE COLLOQUY OF THE TWO SAGES

SALMON OF WISDOM 1

TO THE CELTS THE SALMON SYMBOLIZED GREAT WISDOM:
ITS ARDUOUS, ANNUAL JOURNEY BACK TO ITS BIRTHPLACE
REPRESENTS AN ABILITY TO OVERCOME OBSTACLES
THROUGH DETERMINATION AND INTELLIGENCE.

1 Gaze softly at the entire mandala, let your mind flow like water, and reflect on how life is like a journey, with many challenges along the way.

2 Focus on the intertwined salmon in the centre of the mandala. Follow their tails, which curl around each other, and reflect on how you can both support, and allow yourself to be supported by, the people around you – whether family, friends or colleagues.

3 Consider the ring of knots around the salmon and imagine them using the coiled strength of the fish to break through this barrier. Know that you, too, can draw on your inner strength to help you through hard times.

4 Reflect on the joy and determination of the leaping fish outside the ring of knots. Endeavour to bring these positive qualities into your own life.

RECOMMENDED COLOUR PALETTE

KNOTTED CIRCULAR PATTERNS: **Green** for nature, fertility, charity, prosperity, health
SALMON (colour each scale separately to make a pattern): **Orange** for encouragement, attraction, kindness, plenty; **Yellow** for warmth, confidence, joy, balance; **Green** for nature, fertility, charity, prosperity, health; **Blue** for tranquillity, protection, devotion, sincerity

"UNDERSTANDING IS THE LIGHT OF MANKIND."

MEDIEVAL WELSH TEXT

ENDLESS KNOT WITH CROSS

WELL KNOWN AS A CELTIC SYMBOL, BUT WITH
PARALLELS IN HINDU, BUDDHIST AND CHINESE TRADITIONS,
THE ENDLESS KNOT REPRESENTS INFINITY, THE ENDLESS FLOW OF
TIME AND MOVEMENT, AND THE JOURNEY OF THE PILGRIM.

1 Rest your gaze lightly upon the endless knot in this mandala – the elaborately interlaced thread without a starting point. See this as a transcendental state beyond the material world. Visually trace the thread to satisfy yourself that it has no end.

2 Focus on the central cross within the circle – a symbol of the physical (the cross) fused with the spiritual (the circle).

3 Now let these two images – the encircled cross and the endless knot – enter your mind as a single expression of the eternal truth of existence: all existence is time-bound, but ultimately it rests timelessly within the divine or eternal spirit. Relax in this timelessness throughout your meditation.

RECOMMENDED COLOUR PALETTE

LARGE KNOTWORK: **Green** for nature, fertility, charity, prosperity, health
CIRCULAR TWISTED KNOTS: **Red** for passion, strength, lust
CROSS: **Blue** for tranquillity, protection, devotion, sincerity

"OLD IS MAN WHEN HE IS BORN AND YOUNG, YOUNG EVER AFTER."

TALIESIN

(C.534—C.599 AD)

TRISKELES 1

IN ITS THREE LINKED SPIRALS THE TRISKELE IS TYPICALLY CELTIC,
DENOTING THE SUN, THE AFTERLIFE AND REINCARNATION.
THIS MANDALA MEDITATION MAY ALSO GENERATE
BENEFICIAL ENERGIES IF YOU ARE PREGNANT.

1 Trace in your mind the continuous line of the triple spiral. This, like the endless knot (see page 30), suggests the endless repetition of life's cycles – a life-force restlessly manifesting itself, and the eternity that is implied by such a perspective.

2 Now see this life-force framed within the context of eternal spirit – as reflected in the perfect outer circle of the mandala.

3 Take into your mind this perfect balance of being and becoming, of eternal emptiness and vibrant creation, and let these harmonies radiate through your mind into your nervous system and bloodstream. You are endlessly creative, even as you abide in the stillness of spirit.

RECOMMENDED COLOUR PALETTE

KNOTWORK: **Green** for nature, fertility, charity, prosperity, health
TRISKELES: **Red** for passion, strength, lust; **Orange** for encouragement, attraction, kindness, plenty;
Yellow for warmth, confidence, joy, balance; **Green** for nature, fertility, charity, prosperity, health;
Blue for tranquillity, protection, devotion, sincerity

"GLORY TO YOU, SUN, COUNTENANCE OF THE GOD OF THE ELEMENTS."

TRADITIONAL; COLLECTED BY ALEXANDER CARMICHAEL

(1832—1912)

SACRED BEASTS

CELTIC ART FEATURED HYBRID CREATURES THAT COMBINED AND INTENSIFIED THE ADMIRABLE QUALITIES OF TWO OR MORE REAL ANIMALS. THIS MANDALA CAN HELP YOU TO DEVELOP THESE POSITIVE ENERGIES WITHIN YOURSELF.

1   Look at the mandala as a whole. Keeping your gaze soft and relaxed, let your mind move through the multi-coloured designs. Imagine that each section of the pattern represents a main aspect of your being – something special that makes you unique.

2   Now focus on the strong, lively creatures in the inner circle. Let your eyes follow them as they chase each other in an eternal dance, their constant motion emitting an intense and inspiring energy.

3   Open your mind to the qualities that the hybrid animals might symbolize – such as the courage of lions, the grace of cats and the intelligence of wolves. Identify which of these qualities you would like to embody in your own life and seek to develop these through your daily words, decisions and actions.

RECOMMENDED COLOUR PALETTE

THREE BEASTS: **Green** for nature, fertility, charity, prosperity, health; **Blue** for tranquillity, protection, devotion, sincerity; **Orange** for encouragement, attraction, kindness, plenty

KNOTWORK (top left): **Blue** for tranquillity, protection, devotion, sincerity

KNOTWORK (top right): **Orange** for encouragement, attraction, kindness, plenty

KNOTWORK (bottom left): **Red** for passion, strength, lust

KNOTWORK (bottom right): **Green** for nature, fertility, charity, prosperity, health

"GENEROSITY IS THE KEY TO MARVELS."

THE YELLOW BOOK OF LECAN

THE BEAUTY OF FLOWERS

THE CELTS RECOGNIZED AND PLACED GREAT VALUE ON
THE BEAUTY AND POWER OF PLANTS AND FLOWERS.
WITH THIS MANDALA YOU, TOO, CAN COME TO
APPRECIATE ABUNDANT NATURE IN ALL ITS GLORY.

1 Rest your gaze on the entwined roots at the centre of the mandala – strong and life-giving, yet concealed as they would be in life. Draw a parallel between this and your own invisible life-force, or energy, which is constantly coursing through you and nourishing every cell in your body.

2 Let your eyes travel outward through the circles of interwoven flowers. Notice that the blossoms come in various shapes and sizes, yet each is as beautiful as the next, and they all live in harmony, complementing one another's radiance.

3 Gaze softly upon the whole mandala. Feel the fertile abundance of nature, its splendour and intricacy. Relax, and let your spirit open itself to beauty, like the petals of a flower caressed by sunlight.

RECOMMENDED COLOUR PALETTE

KNOTWORK: **Red** for passion, strength, lust
SHOOTS and LEAVES: **Green** for nature, fertility, charity, prosperity, health
FLOWERS: **Pink** for unity, honour, truth, romance, happiness
BERRIES: **Purple** for piety, sanctity, sentimentality

"HOSPITALITY KEEPS THE FLOWERS ALIVE."

ADAPTED FROM THE COLLOQUY OF THE TWO SAGES

ENDLESS KNOT

THE INTRICATE INTERLACING OF THE CELTIC ENDLESS KNOT
IS A SYMBOL OF THE UNIVERSE AND OF INFINITY –
AN ETERNAL WEB WITHIN WHICH ALL THINGS
ARE INTERCONNECTED.

1 Rest your eyes softly on the interwoven threads, and sense the rhythm and wonder of the endlessly repeating pattern. Consider how this represents the universe at large and the complex web of life.

2 Let your eyes be drawn to any one point in the knot and trace a winding path through the design, over and under the lines as necessary. Follow this path until you return to your starting point.

3 Reflect on how your own life, like this mandala, is a beautiful, constantly evolving pattern of situations and events. Know that everything you do, no matter how small it may seem, adds to the intricate tapestry of your life. Every moment of your existence has its own significance in the wider scheme of things.

RECOMMENDED COLOUR PALETTE

KNOTWORK: **Green** for nature, fertility, charity, prosperity, health;
Blue for tranquillity, protection, devotion, sincerity; **Purple** for piety, sanctity, sentimentality
BLANK SPACES: **Yellow** for warmth, confidence, joy, balance

"WHAT THEN IS TIME? IF NO ONE ASKS ME, I KNOW WHAT IT IS.
IF I WISH TO EXPLAIN IT TO HIM WHO ASKS, I DO NOT KNOW."

ST AUGUSTINE

(354—430 AD)

CELTIC CROSS 2

THE CELTIC CROSS COMBINES TWO POWERFUL SYMBOLS:
THE CIRCLE, SUGGESTING INFINITY OR THE ETERNAL,
AND THE CROSS, SUGGESTING THE WORLD OF PHYSICAL FORMS.
THE IMAGE CAN ALSO BE INTERPRETED AS
A TALISMAN OF CREATIVITY.

1 Look at the two basic forms within the mandala: in essence, the circle suggests the feminine principle and the cross the masculine principle. The interplay of both is all creation.

2 Now move to a higher level of symbolism, seeing the circle as eternity and the cross as the created world. The arms of the cross represent the points of the compass and the four elements.

3 See the fifth element, spirit, as the circle, which also is the circle of life and the endless path of knowledge, all fused into an all-embracing cosmic harmony. Let this harmony enter your mind like water filling a well.

RECOMMENDED COLOUR PALETTE

VERTICAL ARM OF CROSS: **Orange** for encouragement, attraction, kindness, plenty
HORIZONTAL ARM OF CROSS: **Blue** for tranquillity, protection, devotion, sincerity
CENTRAL SWIRLING PATTERN: **Green** for nature, fertility, charity, prosperity, health;
Brown for earth, grounding, talent, telepathy, home;
Blue for tranquillity, protection, devotion, sincerity
OUTER CIRCULAR KNOTWORK: **Red** for passion, strength, lust
BLANK SPACES: **Yellow** (standing in for gold) for energy, wealth, intelligence, longevity

"IF YOU WANT TO UNDERSTAND THE CREATOR,
SEEK TO UNDERSTAND CREATED THINGS."

ST COLUMBANUS

(C.543—615 AD)

SPIRALS

THE CELTS AND OTHER ANCIENT PEOPLES ARE THOUGHT TO HAVE
USED SPIRALS AS SYMBOLS OF THE SUN, SOURCE OF ALL LIFE.
THIS MANDALA REFLECTS THE UNDYING ENERGY OF THE UNIVERSE
– AS WELL AS THE PROGRESS OF THE SOUL.

1 First, see the spirals of the mandala as the dance of divine solar energy, powering all life and all that exists.

2 Now think of the main central spirals as your voyage to enlightenment. Progress toward the still centre at the heart of the self, slowly but surely getting closer. The harmony of this mandala evolves out of our essential goodness as we seek and find the truth.

3 In your mind, fuse these meanings together – the cosmic and the personal. Perceive the two spiral bands of colour as merging into one image that represents the growth of nature and the growth of the soul, the flow of the cosmos and the flow of your own understanding, the creation and dissolution of the world and your own self within the world.

RECOMMENDED COLOUR PALETTE

MAIN CENTRAL SPIRALS (Use two bands of alternating colour): **Orange** for encouragement, attraction,
kindness, plenty; **Blue** for tranquillity, protection, devotion, sincerity
CORNER TRISKELES: **Red** for passion, strength, lust, fertility;
Yellow for warmth, confidence, joy, balance

"THE HUMAN MIND ALWAYS MAKES PROGRESS,
BUT IT IS A PROGRESS IN SPIRALS."

MADAME DE STAËL

(1766—1817)

TRISKELES 2

IN CELTIC TRADITION, THE TRISKELE, COMPRISING THREE RUNNING LEGS CURVING OUT FROM A CENTRAL POINT, EXPRESSES ETERNAL FORWARD MOTION. DRAW ON ITS ENERGY TO HELP YOU TO MOVE SMOOTHLY THROUGH TIMES OF CHALLENGE AND CHANGE.

1 Focus on the large triskele that dominates this mandala. Follow each of the curves as they radiate from the centre, like uncoiling springs. Allow them to awaken your dormant energy.

2 Now bring your attention to the three-pointed knot-work designs around the central one, each spinning in its own orbit. Feel their energy gradually building, as when cells divide. Imagine a similar momentum increasing within your being, empowering you to embrace change and to overcome any obstacles.

3 Shift your gaze through the outer rings of the mandala, feeling the dynamic balance between the swirling energy of the triskeles and the solidity of the traditional knotwork. Trust that you will find the same balance of impetus and security within yourself as you open yourself to change in your life.

RECOMMENDED COLOUR PALETTE

LARGE TRISKELE: **Red** for passion, strength, lust, fertility
CENTRAL SPIRAL S (Use two bands of alternating colour): **Orange** for encouragement, attraction, kindness, plenty; **Blue** for tranquillity, protection, devotion, sincerity
THREE-POINTED KNOTWORK DESIGNS: **Orange** for encouragement, attraction, kindness, plenty
BLANK SPACES: **Yellow** (standing in for gold) for energy, wealth, intelligence, longevity

"THE THREE FOUNDATIONS OF BARDIC KNOWLEDGE:
SONG • BARDIC SECRETS • THE WISDOM WITHIN"

CELTIC TRIAD

PILGRIM'S MAZE

THE LABYRINTH WAS ONCE A SYMBOL OF MORAL CONFUSION,
BUT IN THE MIDDLE AGES CHRISTIANS BEGAN TO SEE IT AS
THE TRUE WAY OF BELIEF. THIS MANDALA IS BASED ON
THE MAZE ON THE FLOOR OF CHARTRES CATHEDRAL, FRANCE.

1 Follow the labyrinth from its entrance (at the bottom) all the way to the floral device at its centre. You should not lose your way because the labyrinth is unicursal – that is, it has no junctions. But if you forget where you are, go back to the start and try again.

2 As you get closer to the centre, imagine travelling deeper and deeper into the self. The labyrinth is your physical incarnation, the life you lead on Earth; and, at the same time, it is the challenges that you face in following your spiritual destiny.

3 Once you reach the centre, view it as a tunnel that leads down into the page. Step into this tunnel. For many the labyrinth continues, but for you the path is now straight – as long as you stay true to the purity of heart that your pilgrimage has brought you.

RECOMMENDED COLOUR PALETTE

LABYRINTH PATH and PAVING: **Brown** for earth, grounding, talent, telepathy, home;
Yellow for warmth, confidence, joy, balance
STAINED-GLASS WINDOWS: **Green** for nature, fertility, charity, prosperity, health;
Yellow for warmth, confidence, joy, balance; **Red** for passion, strength, lust

"O HOW I LONG TO TRAVEL BACK
AND TREAD AGAIN THAT ANCIENT TRACK!"

HENRY VAUGHAN

(1621—1695)

BIRD'S NEST

MANDALAS BASED WHOLLY ON THE NATURAL WORLD HAVE A
UNIVERSAL DIMENSION, FREE OF SPECIFIC CULTURAL SYMBOLISM.
HERE, THE STARTING POINT IS THE ORIGIN OF LIFE EXPRESSED
IN A COMMONPLACE FORM – THE EGG.

1 Look at the elements of the mandala and imagine yourself looking down onto the scene – a bird's nest with three eggs in it right in the centre of a tree's leafy canopy, with four other surrounding nests lower down the tree.

2 Concentrate on the three eggs, first as pure shape and colour. Then lose yourself in the intricate pattern of twigs in the nest.

3 Now begin to imagine the scene as a real, three-dimensional situation. Imagine how high you are above the ground in which the tree is rooted. Imagine the sounds of birdsong all around.

4 Lastly, concentrate on the individual lives cocooned in these three central eggs – the wonder of genetic inheritance, the miracle of nature's ingenuity.

RECOMMENDED COLOUR PALETTE

EGGS: **Blue** for tranquillity, protection, devotion, sincerity
NESTS: **Brown** for earth, grounding, talent, telepathy, home
LEAVES: **Green** for nature, fertility, charity, prosperity, health
LARGE BERRIES: **Orange** for encouragement, attraction, kindness, plenty
SMALL BERRIES: **Red** for passion, strength, lust
BIRDS: **Yellow** for warmth, confidence, joy, balance; **Red** for passion, strength, lust

"I VALUE MY GARDEN MORE FOR BEING FULL OF BLACKBIRDS THAN OF CHERRIES,
AND VERY FRANKLY GIVE THEM FRUIT FOR THEIR SONGS."

JOSEPH ADDISON

(1672—1719)

GREEN MAN

AN ANCIENT PAGAN SYMBOL, THE GREEN MAN IS ALSO FOUND
CARVED ON MEDIEVAL CHURCHES – A REMNANT OF MORE PRIMAL
BELIEFS. HE SYMBOLIZES THE CYCLE OF LIFE, DEATH AND REBIRTH,
AND THE GREEN SAP OF THE LIFE-FORCE.

1   Look at the face camouflaged among the greenery of foliage. Now look closer and notice that leaves are coming out of the man's mouth and flesh – he is an incarnation of nature, not merely an onlooker.

2   Recognize that in many ways we too are incarnations of nature and, conversely, that nature participates in the spirit, in the sense that natural beauty could not exist were it not for our own perception of divine harmony even in the wilderness or wild wood, far from humankind.

3   Take the mandala into your mind as an image of the unity of the cosmos and of our kinship with animals, trees and flowers.

RECOMMENDED COLOUR PALETTE

FACE and FOLIAGE: **Green** for nature, fertility, charity, prosperity, health
ACORN BRANCHES: **Brown** for earth, grounding, talent, telepathy, home
BLANK SPACES: **Yellow** for warmth, confidence, joy, balance

"MAY GOD PROTECT ME – I WRITE WELL IN THE GREENWOOD."

ADAPTED FROM 'A SCRIBE IN THE WOODS'

(C.9TH CENTURY)

SALMON OF WISDOM 2

BECAUSE OF ITS AMAZING ABILITY TO CROSS OCEANS AND FIND ITS WAY UNERRINGLY TO ITS SPAWNING GROUNDS, THE CELTS ASSOCIATED THE SALMON WITH PROPHECY. MEDITATE ON THE SALMON TO COME CLOSER TO YOUR INTUITIVE WISDOM.

1 You are in the branches of a tree looking down. Two salmon are swimming in a circular pool below you. You can see also the leaves of the surrounding trees and the pool's decorative surround. Little hazelnuts are floating on the water's surface: these too are symbolic of prophetic insight.

2 Think of the salmon as a living yin yang symbol: one is male, the other female. Acknowledge both the male and female sides within yourself, as together they give you the gift of insight.

3 Absorb the whole image within yourself. Feel the depths of your intuition. All reason can do is count the fish and the hazelnuts and decorate the pool edge; intuition can penetrate the inner depths, where love and truth are to be found.

RECOMMENDED COLOUR PALETTE

SALMON: **Grey** (standing in for silver) for treasure, values, creativity, inspiration;
Pink for unity, honour, truth, romance, happiness
HAZELNUTS and PEBBLES: **Brown** for earth, grounding, talent, telepathy, home
WATER: **Blue** for tranquillity, protection, devotion, sincerity
FOLIAGE: **Green** for nature, fertility, charity, prosperity, health

"THE SECOND TIME I WAS CREATED, I WAS A BLUE SALMON."

TALIESIN

(C.534—C.599 AD)

NATURE'S HARMONY

CONCENTRIC CIRCLES BRING A SPIRITUAL PURITY TO THIS MANDALA, BASED ON THE ORDER OF THE COSMOS WITH ITS BEAUTIFUL LIFE AND EARTH FORMS. THE FRAME OF THE OUTER CIRCLE EMPHASIZES THE SPIRITUAL DIMENSION.

1 Look at the sky, with its heavenly bodies, in the corners of this mandala. Then progress through the outer frame of lotus motifs. You find yourself symbolically in the realm of the mountains and the clouds.

2 Pass through the next circle into the greenery of nature, where trees, plants, birds and insects abound. This is Eden, the natural paradise.

3 Finally, penetrate to the mystic centre, which borrows from nature to express its divine creativity. Imagine the central circle as the cross-section of a shaft of light that drills into your deepest self to awaken the spirit.

RECOMMENDED COLOUR PALETTE

TREES, LEAVES, SHOOTS and BIRDS: **Green** for nature, fertility, charity, prosperity, health
FLOWERS and BERRIES: **Pink** for unity, honour, truth, romance, happiness
CENTRAL CIRCLE: **Yellow** for warmth, confidence, joy, balance
CLOUDS: **White** for purity, concentration, meditation, peace
MOUNTAINS: **Brown** for earth, grounding, talent, telepathy, home

"FORGET NOT THAT THE EARTH DELIGHTS TO FEEL YOUR BARE FEET AND THE
WINDS LONG TO PLAY WITH YOUR HAIR."

KAHLIL GIBRAN

(1883—1931)

DRAGON KNOTWORK

THE FIRE-BREATHING DRAGON IS FEARFUL AND POWERFUL,
BUT IN THIS MANDALA THE DRAGON'S POWER IS POURED
INTO THE ENDLESS KNOT OF SPIRITUAL PERFECTION.
EARTH AND SPIRIT BLEND IN COSMIC HARMONY.

1   Look at the fire that issues from the four dragons' heads at the top and bottom of the mandala. This is the physical energy of nature, which can become transmuted into spiritual energy. The fire forms a circle – its spiritual character is endless.

2   Now rest your eyes on the dragons' bodies transformed by spirit into an endless knot of eternal perfection. Matter passes into spirit, which purifies it and enfolds it within an all-embracing cosmic harmony – giving birth to the "pearl of great price" in the mandala's centre.

3   Let the mandala become the centre of your awareness and allow the opposites of matter and spirit to blend together, to manifest the wholeness that is our essential nature.

RECOMMENDED COLOUR PALETTE

KNOTWORK OF DRAGONS: **Red** for passion, strength, lust
EYES: **Green** for nature, fertility, charity, prosperity, health;
White for purity, concentration, meditation, peace
FLAMES: **Orange** for encouragement, attraction, plenty
CENTRAL PEARL: **White** for purity, concentration, meditation, peace
ACORNS: **Brown** for earth, grounding, talent, romance, happiness
LEAVES: **Green** for nature, fertility, charity, prosperity, health

"EVERY TRIAL ENDURED AND WEATHERED IN THE RIGHT SPIRIT MAKES A SOUL
NOBLER AND STRONGER THAN IT WAS BEFORE."

W.B. YEATS

(1865—1939)

THE HOLY GRAIL

FOR AN ARTHURIAN KNIGHT, THE HOLY GRAIL MEANT
SELF-KNOWLEDGE, REDEMPTION, IMMORTALITY. HERE THE GRAIL
IS AT THE CENTRE OF THE ROUND TABLE, SURROUNDED BY
THE HELMETS OF THE KING AND SIX OF HIS KNIGHTS.

1   Look, in the lower portion of the mandala, at the sword in the stone, which only the future king can remove. True meditation pulls the sword from the stone, as the physical world becomes subordinate to the spiritual.

2   Recognize that the king, at the head of the table, is a symbol of yourself. The knights around you are your personal qualities. See yourself as inwardly protected by armour and magic shields. Name each one by one.

3   Lastly, feel worthy to approach the Grail, which is empty yet at the same time full of love. Imagine yourself holding the Grail and feeling its transforming power.

4   Contemplate the four castles – representing the inner strength of a life well lived, the impregnability of the spirit in the face of change and challenge.

RECOMMENDED COLOUR PALETTE

GRAIL, HELMETS, KNOTS, CASTLES and SWORD: **Grey** (standing in for silver)
for treasure, values, creativity, inspiration
CIRCLE OF SHIELDS: **Brown** for earth, grounding, talent, telepathy, home.
Alternatively, colour each shield intuitively, or following traditional symbolism
KNOTWORK DESIGNS: **Blue** for tranquillity, protection, devotion, sincerity

"HE WILL WIPE EVERY TEAR FROM THEIR EYES. THERE WILL BE NO MORE DEATH
OR MOURNING OR CRYING OR PAIN, FOR THE OLD ORDER OF THINGS
HAS PASSED AWAY."

REVELATION 21:4

THE WORLD'S WEATHER

THE WEATHER IS A SYMBOL OF ENDLESS CHANGE.
IT OFFERS A LESSON IN ACCEPTANCE: IF WE FIND IT DIFFICULT TO
ACCEPT THE WEATHER REGARDLESS OF ANY PLANS WE HAVE MADE,
WE HAVE A LONG WAY TO GO IN OUR SPIRITUAL JOURNEY.

1 Look at the suns, which are shown in each of the four corners of this mandala. The sun is always there, driving life's energies, even when obscured by cloud. In the same way, our identity and our spirit are unaltered by shifts of fortune.

2 Now concentrate on the mandala's depiction of clouds, rain, rainbows, snow and rough seas. All this weather belongs to one vast self-regulating global system, which the mandala as a whole symbolizes.

3 Lastly, focus on the central point of the mandala – the still source of the endless streams of energy that bring all weathers and all other changes into the cosmos. This is the energy from which we are made. Take the mandala deep into your mind where that energy finds its still centre.

RECOMMENDED COLOUR PALETTE

SUNS: **Yellow** for warmth, confidence, joy, balance;
Orange for encouragement, attraction, kindness, plenty
ROUGH SEAS: **Blue** for tranquillity, protection, devotion, sincerity
RAIN: **Grey** for neutrality, cancelling, balance
MOUNTAINS: **Green** for nature, fertility, charity, prosperity, health
CLOUDS: **White** for purity, concentration, meditation, peace
RAINBOWS: **Colours of the Rainbow** for benevolence, growth, energy

"UNDERSTANDING IS THE LIGHT OF MANKIND."

ADAPTED FROM A MEDIEVAL WELSH MANUSCRIPT

ARCHES OF THE HEAVENS

THE DOME OF A TEMPLE OR CHURCH IS OFTEN MANDALA-LIKE
WHEN SEEN FROM BELOW – A PATTERN MADE UP OF THE ARCHES
OF WINDOWS AND CRISS-CROSSING ROOF SUPPORTS.
THE RESULTING VIEW, OF COURSE, IS HEAVENWARD.

1   Pick out the main features of the mandala – the view directly upward into an elaborate dome. The three-dimensional geometry is complex, but don't try to decipher each decorative or structural element, just absorb the basic architecture, and the four decorative flower motifs.

2   Imagine sunlight passing through the windows of the dome and bringing it to life, in the same way that sunlight gives life to living beings.

3   Think of the image as a two-dimensional pattern again, and take it deep into your mind – you are now contemplating the heavens and the life-affirming light of divinity. You are peacefully at prayer – although you are asking for nothing.

RECOMMENDED COLOUR PALETTE

CENTRAL FLOWER and CURVED WINDOW SECTIONS: **Blue** for tranquillity,
protection, devotion, sincerity
FOUR FLOWER MOTIFS: **Green** for nature, fertility, charity, prosperity, health
OUTER CURVED BLANK SPACES: **Yellow** (standing in for gold) for energy, wealth, intelligence, longevity

"TRUE WORSHIP IS SEEKING TO UNITE THE SPIRIT BELOW
WITH THE SPIRIT ABOVE."

CELTIC APHORISM

(2ND CENTURY BC—1ST CENTURY AD)

DRAGON BREATHING FIRE

THE DRAGON IS THE PARADOX OF BEING – LIGHT AND DARK,
CREATION AND DESTRUCTION, MALE AND FEMALE, AND THE
UNIFYING FORCE OF THESE OPPOSITES. THE DRAGON'S FIRE
IS THE PRIMAL ENERGY OF THE PHYSICAL WORLD.

1 Look at the mandala's seven-headed dragon and imagine its overwhelming, invincible power. Trace this power in the ring of flames. Nothing more awesome can be imagined in all the universe.

2 The seven heads symbolize the mystical number of the cosmos. They are the sum of the number of divinity (three) and the number of humankind (four).

3 Finally, concentrate on the knot of dragons' necks at the centre of the mandala. This is where all contradictions are resolved. See this knot as the endless cycle of being, infinitely dynamic in its surge of limitless power.

RECOMMENDED COLOUR PALETTE

DRAGONS: **Green** for nature, fertility, charity, prosperity, health
FLAMES: **Orange** for encouragement, attraction, plenty; **Red** for passion, strength, lust
CIRCLE OF ROCKS: **Grey** for neutrality, cancelling, balance
BACKGROUND WITHIN CIRCLE: **Blue** for tranquillity, protection, devotion, sincerity

"LIKE A SPECKLED SERPENT WITH A CREST, ONE HUNDRED SINFUL SOULS ARE
PUNISHED IN HIS FLESH."

TALIESIN

(C.534—C.599 AD)

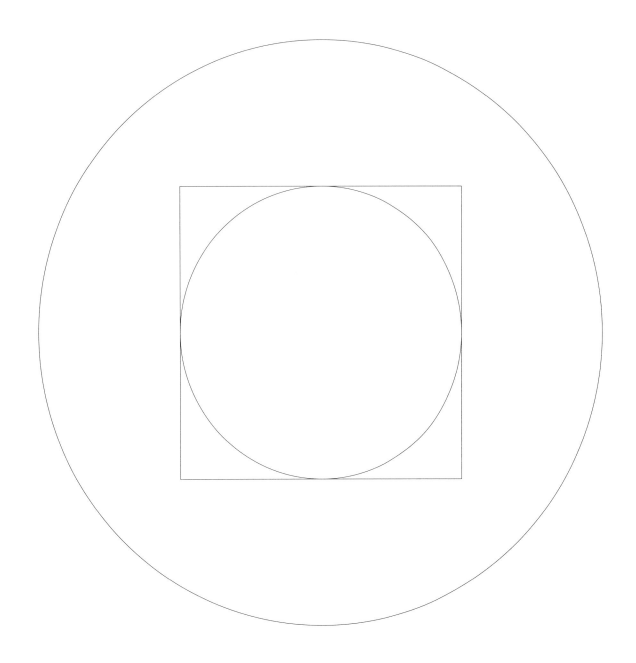

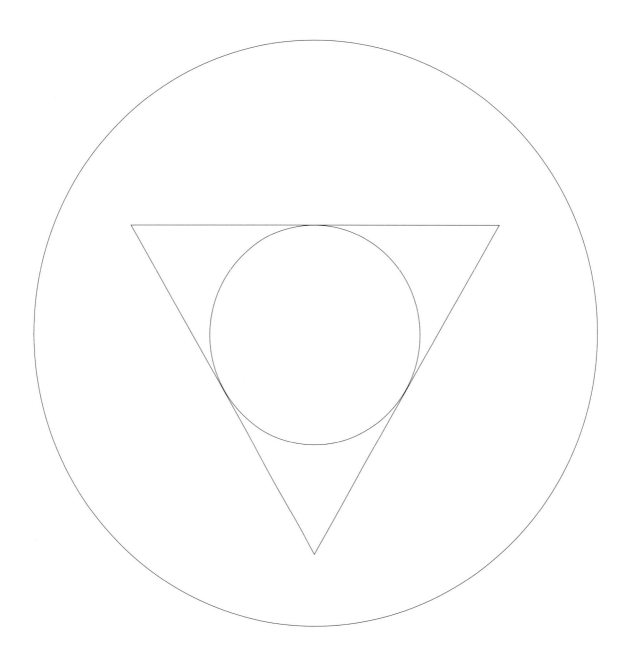

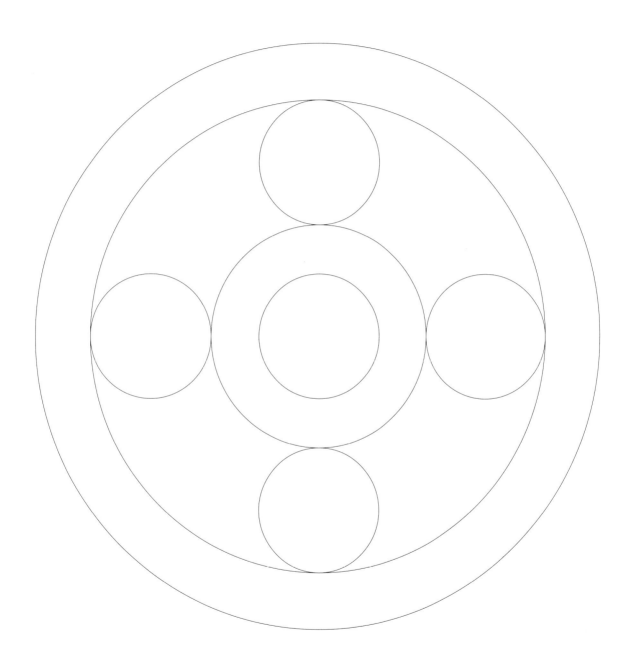

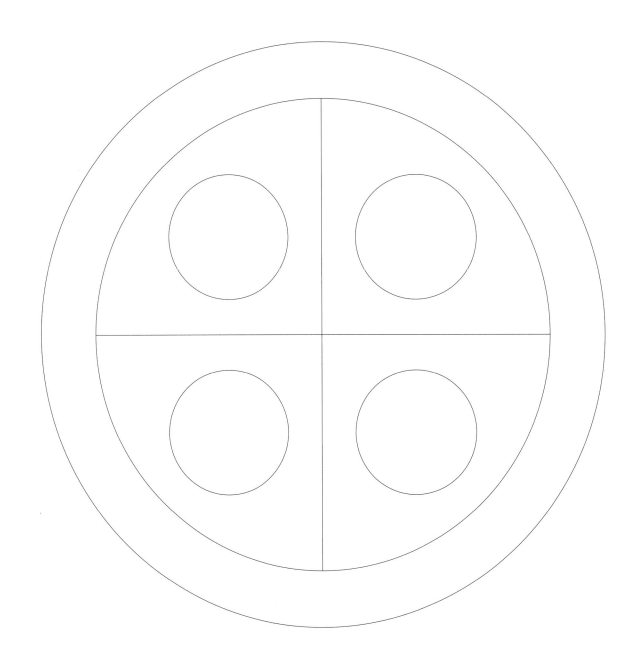

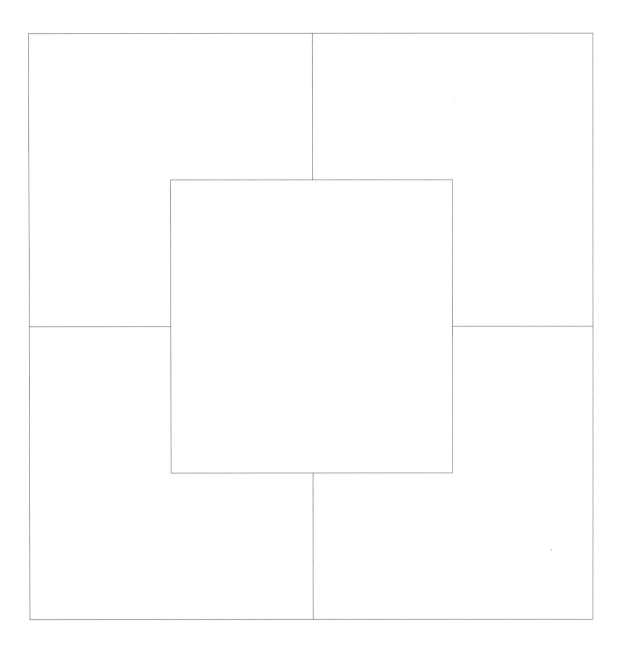

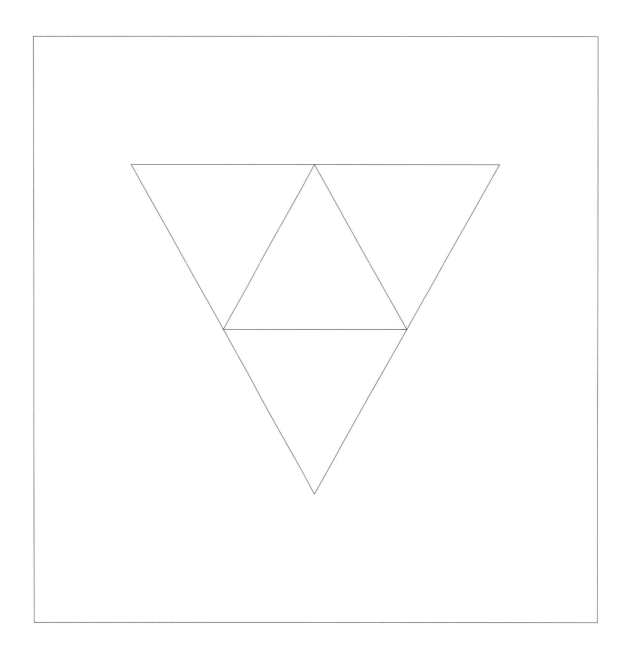

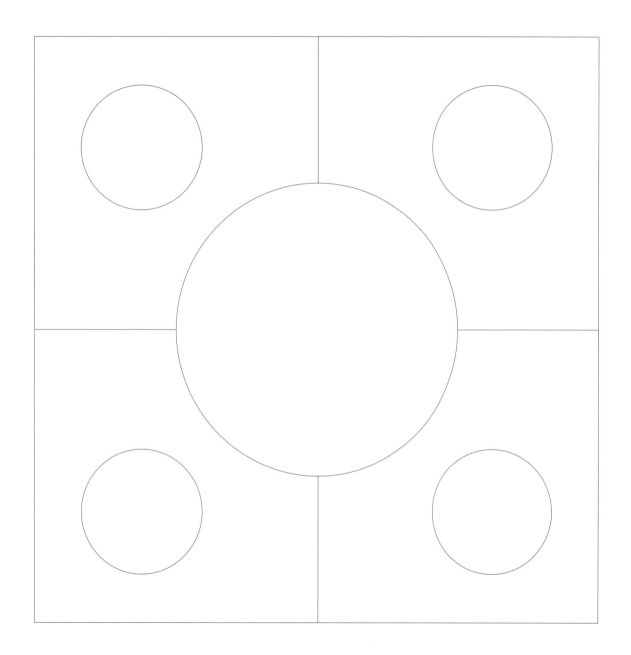

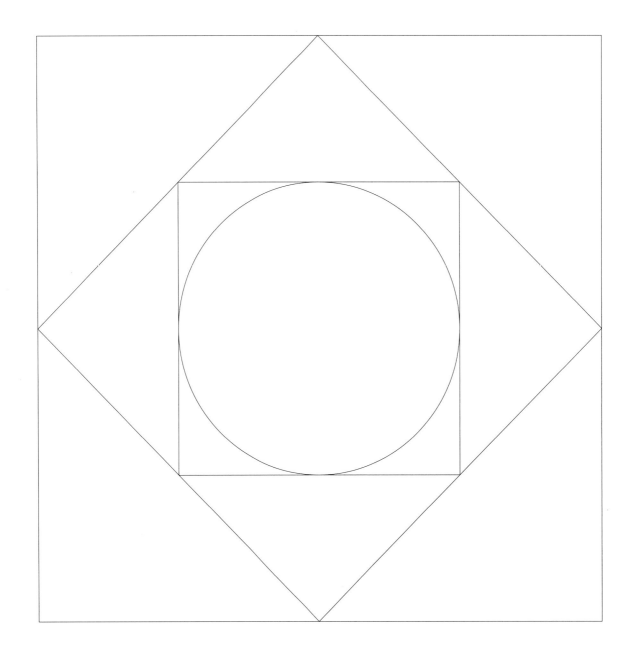

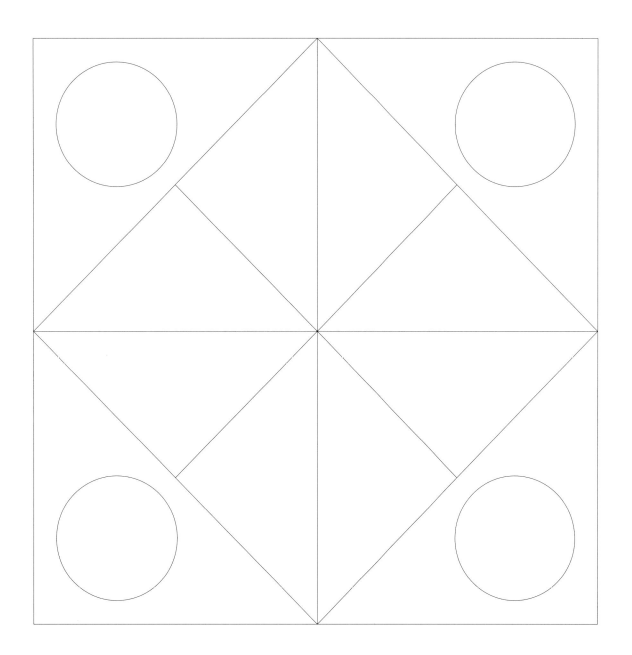

INSPIRATIONS FROM NATURE

The Celts showed a great respect for nature: they held their rituals in woodland groves, and regarded springs, rivers and wells as places of healing and renewal. Nature was the fabric that underpinned the Celtic way of life, and nowhere was the wisdom, respect and spirituality of this passionate people more apparent than in their extraordinary artwork, which was vibrant with colour and symbolism that evoked the energy flowing through all of creation. The Tree of Life, with its deep roots and lush branches, was a particularly potent symbol, depicting the connection between the earthly and spiritual realms.

A great variety of plants was used by the Celts in their medicine as well as in religious celebrations. Mistletoe and oak were particularly sacred, while hazelnuts were said to bestow wisdom and insight. The great significance of plants is evident in the way they were interwoven in different styles of artwork – whether engraved in jewelry, weapons and stones, or used to elaborate the written word.

Animals and birds, too, played a prominent role in Celtic art and myth. Their fertility was a reminder of the cycles of life, and certain creatures were seen as spiritual guides. Each conferred its own valuable qualities – for example, *boars* represented strength and courage in war, while *stags* denoted the Horned God, Cernunnos, who was associated with fertility and masculinity. *Horses* were a particularly strong symbol, representing freedom, power, fertility and nobility. They also signified healing, and were thought to bring messages to people in dreams. Even more significant are two creatures that feature in the mandalas in this book: the *dragon*, denoting elemental powers; and the *salmon*, suggesting prophecy or intuition. You can use any of these as "power animals" by focusing on them and calling on their special qualities before you begin to work with a mandala, or while you meditate on one.

Another important and widespread Celtic motif inspired by nature was the spiral, symbolizing the never-ending cycle of the natural world, and thus also suggesting open-ended possibilities and progress. The circle, a fundamental shape in mandalas, features in the traditional form of the Celtic labyrinth – a winding path cut into the ground, which people followed as a journey toward their own spiritual centre. The Star in the Well, opposite, shows a simplified version of this idea.

The mandalas in this book provide insight into the Celtic world and allow you to tap into the deep spirituality of these people: they also offer the chance for an inward journey to find your wise, inner self, and the peace that such discovery will bring you.

DIRECTORY OF CELTIC MANDALA SYMBOLS

Written records left by the Celts are scant, so the origins and meanings of their symbols have often proved difficult to determine. Much of what we know has come to us by way of the Romans, who conquered the Celtic lands during the rise of their Empire. On these pages is a selection of symbols that are Celtic either in essence or in atmosphere. Popular motifs include the endless knot, which represents the interminable crossings of the spiritual and physical paths in our lives; and the Celtic cross, which is probably the most widely recognized of all Celtic symbols. The Green Man and the dragon both testify to the Celtic fascination with elemental power. One of the most influential bodies of Celtic iconography comes from the mythical tales about King Arthur and the Knights of the Round Table, and the search for the Holy Grail – supposedly a respository of Christ's blood after the Crucifixion. This blend of ancient myth and later Christian associations that were interfused with the native tradition during the Middle Ages is one of the most compelling aspects of the Celtic world-view.

Bird's Nest
Strong yet delicate, the bird's nest symbolizes nurture – our home in the wilderness.

Endless Knot
With no beginning and no end, the Celtic knot reminds us of eternity and spiritual perfection.

Leaves
Some leaves are able to grow among rocks, symbolizing a long and lasting friendship.

Dome
The celestial canopy, given concrete form in sacred archi-tecture, is a universal archetype.

Chalice
This receptacle for life-giving water has overtones of intuition and psychic ability.

Labyrinth
A cryptic pattern of pathways, taking us on a journey to the centre of our own being.

Sunrise
Symbolizes new beginnings
and the passage from darkness
(ignorance) into light (faith).

Green Man
A pagan nature spirit, which
symbolizes our oneness with
nature – our groundedness.

Triskele
A three-part spiral, signifying
dynamism and spiritual
progress.

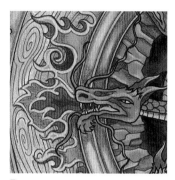

Dragon
An embodiment of cosmic
energy, associated with the four
elements.

Cross
Although the Celtic Cross is
more common (see p.3), here is
a cross of leaves and berries.

Salmon
Primarily associated with
wisdom and prophecy, the
salmon is deeply spiritual.

Rose
Highly ambiguous, the rose
symbolizes both heavenly
perfection and earthly passion.

Acorns
A symbol of longevity and
perseverance, associated with
the Druids.

Swirling Water
Water has universal associations
with purity. Its fluidity is also
representative of the life-cycle.

CELTIC MANDALAS
LISA TENZIN-DOLMA

First published in the UK and USA in 2013 by
Watkins Publishing Limited
Sixth Floor
75 Wells Street
London W1T 3QH

A member of Osprey Group

Osprey Publishing Inc.
43-01 21st Street
Suite 220B, Long Island City
New York 11101

Editor: Rebecca Sheppard
Managing Designer: Sailesh Patel
Commissioned Artwork: mandala colour artworks
by Sally Taylor/ArtistPartners Ltd; line illustrations
for mandala templates by Studio 73

IBSN: 978-1-78028-601-3

10 9 8 7 6 5 4 3 2 1

Typeset in Novecento wide, Filosofia and Gill Sans
Colour reproduction by PDQ, UK
Printed in China

Publisher's note: This book does not recommend
meditation with mandalas for the specific treatment
of any disability, only for the enhancement of general
well-being. Meditation is beneficial for most people
and generally harmless, but those unsure of its suitability
for them should consult a medical practitioner before
attempting any of the meditations in this book. Neither
the publishers nor the author can accept responsibility
for any injuries or damage incurred as a result of
following the meditations in this book, or using any of
the meditation techniques that are mentioned herein.